SPEAKING FLAME

by the same author

poetry

WINTER SCARECROW
MASKS AND FACES
EVIDENCE
HOMAGE TO TOUKARAM
THE FABIUS POEMS
A FULL CIRCLE
NO DIAMONDS, NO HAT, NO HONEY
LOVE'S FIRE: RE-CREATIONS OF RUMI

translations
(with Anne Pennington)

MACEDONIAN SONGS
BLAZHE KONESKY (SELECTED POEMS)
THE GOLDEN APPLE

fiction

ONE LAST MIRROR
BURNING HOUSES
THE WEB

non-fiction

A JOURNEY IN LADAKH

SPEAKING FLAME

RUMI

re-created by
ANDREW HARVEY

Meeramma
Ithaca, New York USA

Meeramma Publications
26 Spruce Lane
Ithaca, New York 14850
USA

Printed in USA

ISBN 0-9622973-1-3

Cover by Christine Cox

Library of Congress Cataloging-in-Publication Data

Jalāl al-Dīn Rūmī, Maulana, 1207-1273.
    [Selections. English. 1989]
    Speaking flame / Rumi : re-created by Andrew Harvey
        p.   cm.
    ISBN 0-9622973-1-3 : $8.95
    1. Sufi poetry, Persian—Translations into English.   2. English
poetry—Translations from Persian.   I. Harvey, Andrew, 1952-
II. Title.
PK6480.E5H37   1989b
891'.5511—dc20   89-39444
                                                           CIP

for Mother Meera

Introduction

Rumi lived and wrote in Turkey during the thirteenth century, in a society very different from ours, but his message—of a transcendent Love that burns away all barriers between man and God and man and man—has never been more urgent. In a world ravaged by division, by fundamentalism of all kinds, religious and political, Rumi's voice, raised in honour of a Love that leaps over all lesser half-truths and convictions, is one of that handful of illumined voices by which human beings must now be guided to preserve the future.

Rumi received the highest mystical illuminations; they showed him the oneness of his and all men's Identity with God and that the end of life was to embody this Identity in active joy. Although a Sufi and a moslem, Rumi honoured all paths to Enlightenment and held all religions sacred. Konya, where he lived for more than fifty years, stood on the ancient silk route, a crossroads where buddhists, christians, and hindus as well as moslems met and exchanged beliefs freely. When he died, Rumi was mourned by every religious denomination as a great poet and spiritual Master. Few men have left to those who came after them so luminous a Sign of what it means to live in Truth beyond the consolations of dogma, in complete exposure to the rigour of Love. The world has never needed that Sign so much, or the poetry that flamed from Rumi's communion with God, whose range, poignance, passion, sense of tender boundlessness few other mystics in the world's literature, if any, can match.

Most of the poems in this book have been adapted from Rumi's Rubaiyat, a collection of quatrains. Some have been 're-created' from his Discourses or Mathnawi. The majority were inspired by Rumi's adoration for his Master, Shams I Tabriz. There are one hundred and eight poems, because 108 is the sacred number of the East and the number of beads on a rosary. I have organised them into a verbal 'raga' that begins in agonised appeal to the Divine, shifts into the experience of Presence and ends in a prolonged, many-sided joy of Enlightenment. Each poem should be read on its own and then as part of this musical and mystical expansion.

To attempt to 're-create' in another language and at another time the vision of a spiritual genius like Rumi demands an effort to participate in that vision. I have been on a journey with a Master. This book is dedicated to Her.

I have worked over several years from the original Persian with help from friends and scholars and glosses in many European languages. What I have striven for is a fusion between the directness of English and the

abandon of Persian, between Rumi's imagination, and
Quest, and my own.

Andrew Harvey
Thalheim '89

Total reversal; this world becomes ghostly
This sun a ghost sun to your Sun...
Pale with terror and awe, I stagger
Between dimensions, fleeing my shadow.

In this old house
The rain has rotted
My heart is in ruin—
Love, enter, or let me leave.

Longing for you savages me each moment
Let the world be my killer, not you
Don't kick the man you sent sprawling in the dust
Don't kill him you made, for the first time, alive.

Heart, you are lost; but there's a path
From the lover to the soul, secret
But visible. Worlds blaze round you—
Don't shrink; the path's secret, but yours.

Run forward, the way will spring open to you
Be destroyed, you'll be flooded with life
Humble yourself, you'll grow greater than the world
Yourself will be revealed to you, without you.

'Blood must flow' he said
'For the garden to flower
And the heart that loves me
Is a wound without shield'

Stop learning, start knowing.
The rose opens, opens
And when it falls
Falls outward.

You are the Sea of fire; we, your foam
Flaming, falling with each wave. . .
Beat us, Lord, with hands bloody with love
We gape between your hands like a drum.

You rest in my arms like a lute
I sing for you like a lover.
You want to break this mirror?
Take this stone.

Yesterday he came to me
I shouted 'Go away'
Grace danced towards me
I shut my door.

Battered; ill; aghast—
Lost in my own ruin—
Sometimes I am weak enough
To enter you.

Whatever grief longing for him brings
Whatever blood Love mixes in his wine
Be grateful; there's one worse fate—
Never seeing him once.

Become the prey of God and be freed from grief
Enter your own being, hurt holds you captive
Know your life throws a veil over your path
Linger with yourself, you'll only grow exhausted.

My only safety; this shaky soaring
That skins all hope, all desire. . .
All I am is a bead on your string
Keep turning me with one finger.

Sometimes a grief like storm-wind sweeps away
All the words I found to bring to you
I shake helpless, silent as a corpse
'Be happy' you say 'Now you are nothing'

How do I live when you're not here?
Pain lives me, a wound speaks with my mouth.
And when you return? Only you know
How you hollow me out and dance in the hollow.

I ran to him. 'I've missed you' he said.
Liar! Then: 'I want your life'
He can have it, but not for a few days.
It's worth nothing; I just want him to beg.

My heart sank smoking into your heart's inferno
The world's stream flashed with your flame-water. . .
Split-second vision that burned away reason
If I was dreaming, I will die

When for a second I am the soul he loves
I shatter the worlds.
Unlovable, hard, in misery,
I tear myself from earth like a tree.

Suddenly, the face of the world grows dim
The Beloved appears from behind his veil
How my heart shivers and burns for Him!
All the nine heavens shine sad with love

Today, this once, my Beloved, don't go, accept
This frail tattered flower, this thorn-on-fire
Take in, coquette, this sad-eyed shabby client
Embrace, flawless full moon, my boiling darkness

Seizing my life in your hands, you thrashed it clean
On the savage rocks of Eternal Mind.
How its colours bled, until they grew white!
You smile and sit back; I dry in your sun.

Hope for the death of hope
The Bird of Paradise is born
From the ashes of illusion
Bird with your wings and Eye of Fire

A tumult of drunkenness
Falls from heaven
Falling from this height
Breaks the world apart.

Seize the diamond knife of purified fury
Slash your way out of the circus-cage of Reason
Murder the liar in you and drag his corpse
Where the other rational corpses can smell their stink.

Dare to throw your being at the Beloved's feet
Cling, day and night, to the circle of lovers
Leave your life in ashes and run to this fervour
Stand trembling by the Creator, fire by Fire.

Enemies say 'We always knew he was stupid'
God knows I must seem so, saying nothing
But your name, weeping like a madwoman
When you're here, when you've gone.

If in hell I could hold one curl of your hair
I'd think the saints of heaven in torment
Called, without you, to the fields of Paradise
Their widest splendours would seem narrow.

Hammer this heart any way you like
For the right ringing sounds
To spread like water
Over the dry listening dead.

Sometimes fury shoots from me, sometimes love,
I never know which face you'll show
Who lives in me now and dangles my body
Whatever way you want until I die.

Beyond my will, words race from my lips
I get no real news of him who speaks
Sometimes I want poison, sometimes sugar
What do I know of what I am or do?

'You'll not have escaped from yourself
Until your Light is a thousand times you'
I could not know what he meant
Before he exploded me

Beauty harsher than a thousand suns
Broke into my house, asked 'How is your heart?'
His robe of glory trailed the floor; I said
'Pick up your robe; the house is floored with blood'

This Fire I crackle in is You
I burn as You, burning away myself...
Mad lucidities! Triumphs without sound!
Don't look for me; I am not here.

He has arrived, He's with us
A thousand secret flames are dancing.
You laugh? You do not know yourself
You could not laugh and know yourself.

I pull you to me by a knowledge beyond words
You think we're meeting for the first time?
I know Him in you, I see you completely
You've eaten His food; the crumbs are on your lips.

My Rock, my Flower, Flower-Rock, Rock-Flower
Dancer-Who-Does-Not-Move! Changeless Eruption!
You sever my head, and Mind grows radiant:
Push me underwater; Heart learns to talk.

Patience makes my soul and robe burn
Mine; everyone's.
I say your name; my mouth breaks into flame—
The two worlds blaze.

The Fire is one, one only, one always
Bird beating red wings in each thing that lives
I am not a voice, I am the Fire singing
What you hear is crackling in you

What I tell about 'me' I tell about you
The walls between us long ago burned down
This voice seizing me is your voice
Burning to speak to us of us

All my splendour is to burn in you
To know this Fire that eats me
Is eating itself, to be this Fire
Dancing on my own bones

You brought me Eternal Light
In your body's burning cup
Laughing as I drank
And grew wings of Fire

'I am nothing' you said. That nothing
Makes the cosmos a ghost.
'I've nothing in my hand but dust'
Nebulae jostle for that dust.

You are 'there', I 'here'. Worlds separate us,
Death's angels, the void of space. . .
Yet I say your name, and waves of Light
Wash to me silently from your Heart.

My hard eyes broke and grew a rose
Whose one huge eye saw only you
Flowering in cosmos after cosmos
Laughing as we grew

I wept my life away and learned to live
Where tears are prayers, all stumbling
Dancing to the drum of suns, these cries
Sounds of extreme love

You've given me your terrible Double Eye
That sees all things as empty and as You.
You scathe all flesh to bone, flame bone to Light
How could I survive such horror, and splendour?

'If I die' I said 'Who will speak to you
Of You?' He smiled 'Die, I'll speak through you
Words so fierce, so dangerous with love
No-one who hears them will live long'

What you see of me is only
What you know of yourself
I left these words long ago
To dance round my ghost

Drunk on the milky light of the stars
Anyone staggers. If I seem mad
I am. And if you see that
You are too. Be glad.

No stain of hope or illusion
Your Lightning does not whiten...
I was proud; I'm playing like a child
Walked so straight; am one smoking zig-zag

I am not sane. Who could see you
And stay sane, or want to?
This Fire eating me eats you
This Fire I speak speaks you

This world is now the blood in my veins
How can blood sleep? It has to pump through . . .
My veins dance burning with the blood of madness
The final laughter of the Magician.

Cosmic comedian! Giving me smilingly
All I ever asked for
Passion, Vision, Truth-knowing
They would kill me.

Look to dance for Him, not for peace, and peace
Bleeds into your feet from the dance's truth
Even in terror adamantine laughter
Drums out the secret of who you are

All tracks vanished; you said 'Travel on'
I turned to beg you stay; you had gone.
Winds pressed round me, that smelled of you
Small flowers blossomed, words from your mouth.

Life flows out; he pours you another cup.
The wine? Eternal love.
His wine in me sings this:
His wine flows between us like blood.

This music erupts from my heaven
This fragrance from my garden—
This thing in my soul, my soul—
Where could it run? It is mine.

My best days are when I melt
Love streams from me
Warm, timeless, honey
From your invisible comb

Each awakening soul, O love, is alerted to your news
Each being falls asleep on the breast of your grace
Apart from you, nothing hidden or manifest exists
Each word I try to add, awe wraps in silence

You threw me the world
I caught it, threw it back...
Who was throwing what to whom?
Whose hands are these, burning?

Do you know what night does?
Night separates lovers from strangers.
Tonight with the full moon in my house
The moon is passionate, I am mad.

Mad winter night...
Fire in all the rooms...
All of us mad, on fire...
Who will ever sleep again?

The sea boils with passion for you
The clouds pour pearls at your feet.
A lightning from your love has pierced the earth
This smoke curling to heaven is its child.

In the sea of love, I melt like salt
Faith, Doubt—they both dissolve.
A star is opening in my heart
The worlds turn in it.

With one silent laugh
You tilted the night
And the garden ran with stars.

Your Light burned away my last illusion
The world and I died together
I woke a ghost smiling among ghosts
Unreal and gentle in a world of You

I thought the world real until you laughed
Walls fell, then reared again
Transparent now, soft dancing fans
You shut, and open, when you want

So often I put up my hands
To shield my eyes from you
Wild hilarious miracle!
Your Light shines through my bones

Sometimes in all this talk I find a word
With your mark on it
In the blood of love.
And the worlds go quiet.

Each being is your gold, walking
Love the eyes that see the gold.
Last night I touched your beauty
Woke, an alchemist.

We were green; we ripened and grew golden.
The Sea terrified us; we learned how to drown.
Squat and earthbound, we unfolded huge wings.
We started sober; are Love's startled drunkards.

I watch you dancing in all my actions
Without using eyes, I spy you at play
My old eyes wore thin, I threw them away
Vision grew in their sockets like grass

I know nothing; pass away; only you live on
Passing my moods like masks before your face
Dancing through my skull your wordless secret
Rattling its jewel in this bowl of bone

The truth so simple
The mind explodes
To meet itself
Running back in all things

'The One is pure and silent
Why go on talking?'
The most radiant in me
Has never said a word.

This mystery; I walk towards you
You well up shining in me;
Speak this, loudly—
Hear nothing but Sea

These webs of smouldering silk
You throw round me each moment
Hide everything, hide nothing—
Your eyes in mine see through.

Tears at your tender glory
Surprise me in each alley
I begged to go mad; I have!
You've made my eyes a Sea

Dawn! At last! Atoms are whirling
Souls dancing without head or feet.
Who are they dancing for? I'll show you—
And where the dance is dragging him.

Nothing in my ears but your love's murmur
Eternity's sweetness leaves no reason alive
Love-without-colour mixes colours marvellously
I wear the void's white; death drains from me.

I have seen death with his face:
Heard death singing with his voice
Songs that bring suns into my mouth,
Burn all words to vision.

I unstoppered the wine jar, its fragrance flowed
Into all streets and quarters of the city
Under its knife the blood of hearts flowed like
   water
The fragrance swam back to its jar, still fresh

You are my death, my love, and dying you
I live in deep calm waves of bliss
That wash me past all worlds
To break in Origin

No-one ever sees that last moment
The eroded rock becomes sand
But if they did they would hear
The Sea singing

Find the real world, give it endlessly away
Grow rich, fling gold to all who ask
Live at the empty heart of Paradox
I'll dance there with you, cheek to cheek

Your Dawn in me. . . I'm drunk, stammering—
A thousand thousand words go dark—
Lightnings are dark—to us—to this:
Identity's boundless worlds-wide blaze

From your heart to mine, secret after secret
Whose is this talk that needs no words?
A diamond tree blossoms in Nothingness
The bird of Nowhere never stops singing

This miracle, daily as dawn and sundown,
Normal as bread, as sleep after love:
If I look at him, I see my own image
If I look at my own, I see his, aflame

To meet my thousand thousand faces
I roam my world; the dirtiest grass
Wears the sunlight of my skin:
I stand in this stream, myself, and laugh.

Live to give everything away
So nothing keeps us apart
Love brings you here; Light-atom pulsing
Always, at the Sun's heart.

Your eyes opened in mine; I saw
Your snow-Light soaking every garden.
Your ears bloomed in mine; I heard
Your river running over every stone.

Beauty and Love are as body and soul:
Inexhaustible mine, and diamond-beyond-price.
I loved his Beauty and Love flamed from me:
I grew beautiful, Love whispered my name.

I am trampled grapes
Run where Love pulls me
'Why whirl round me?' you laugh
I'm whirling round myself

I live in him, am him, am him-as-me
Living as me, with me, as me-with-him
Ecstasy makes pronouns swim
Snows melt; gardens start swarming

One night he said 'You are my spring:
All these worlds are blossoming
In you' I staggered: saw
Each nebula my flower

Leaping up onto the roof
My head split open
On the moon.
Crying for joy: not a sound

You hide me in your cloak of Nothingness
Reflect my ghost in your glass of Being
I am nothing, yet appear: transparent dream
Where your Eternity briefly trembles

Reconciled to myself, I emerge into the world
Bare of all thought, clear love in which
The sun on my doorstep dances to your drum
The ant walking into it is no less than You

Wild, peaceful, days where the slightest wind
Soars perfumed with your traces. . .
I am in a heaven of One
Unable to talk, not to talk

No-one will know me until they climb
Where I and they are no more
Final Mountain where mind goes white
To melt in garden after garden

No Heaven or earth, just this mysterious place
We walk in dazedly, where being here
Or there, in time or not, are only
Two motions of the same ecstatic breathing

When Love is in me, I am One with Love
The lightning when I say your name
I roam a dazzled drunkard in our dimension
Where each event is secret laughter

The image in the mirror seems different
But sublime days arrive when you know
Viewer, image, and mirror are one: the same
Silent calm eternal shimmering

One Moon blossoming in a thousand bowls
One Water laughing in a thousand thousand fields
One Sun with a million electric shadows
One Silence with these love-cries for children

Great tree of bliss! Your swaying braziers
Musk each second with Eternity!
I wade incessantly your sea of star-flowers
Your trunk soars blazing from my heart

I have shrunk beyond the smallest atom
Expanded further than the last star
All that is left of Rumi is only
This garden laughing with fruit

The law of Wonder rules my life at last
I burn each second of my life to love
Each second of my life burns out in love
In each leaping second love lives afresh